My Pet Fish

My Pet Fish

by **Lori Coleman**
photographs by **Jerry Boucher**

L Lerner Publications Company • Minneapolis

For Piper—L.C.

Acknowledgments
The author wishes to thank Lee Engfer, Jerry Boucher, Leif, Barb, Stefan, Sture, and Bjorn Berg, Chad Needham, Ted LeVin, Bob Edstrom, and all the fish for their invaluable contributions to this book.

The following photographs are by: p. 12 (top), Jim Simondet; p. 45 (top), © Tom McHugh, Steinhart Aquarium/Photo Researchers; p. 50 (left), p. 51 (right), © Patrice Ceisel/Visuals Unlimited; p. 56 (top), © Tom McHugh/Photo Researchers. The illustrations on pages 10 and 19 are by Laura Westlund.

Website address: www.lernerbooks.com

Library of Congress Cataloging-in-Publication Data

Coleman, Lori, 1967–
  My pet fish / by Lori Coleman; photographs by Jerry Boucher.
    p. cm. – (All about pets)
  Includes bibliographical references and index.
  Summary: Twelve-year-old Leif gives information about choosing and caring for pet fish, setting up and maintaining an aquarium, and dealing with other fishkeeping issues.
    ISBN 0–8225–2262–4 (alk. paper)
    1. Aquarium fishes—Juvenile literature. 2. Aquariums—Juvenile literature. [1. Aquarium fishes. 2. Fishes. 3. Aquariums. 4. Pets.] I. Boucher, Jerry, 1941– ill. II. Title. III. Series.
  SF457.25.C65 1998
  639.34—dc21   98–10861

Manufactured in the United States of America
1 2 3 4 5 6 – JR – 03 02 01 00 99 98

Contents

Fish are peaceful and fun to watch...

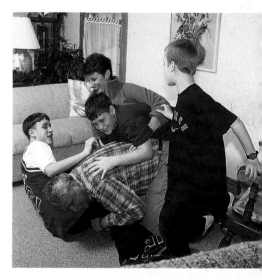

Life in my family gets pretty wild sometimes, like when we all get into a "monkey pile" and wrestle. When I need a break, I go into my room and look at my fish.

"Mom!" Stefan yelled. "Bjorn kicked me again!"

"No, I didn't," said Bjorn. "But it's hard to walk around you when you're sprawled out in the middle of the room."

My name is Leif, and Bjorn and Stefan are my brothers. Stefan is the youngest—he's only eight. I just turned 12, and Bjorn is 14. It's not always easy being one of three boys in the house. Sometimes it gets pretty loud.

When I want some peace and quiet, I usually go to my room. That's where most of my fish aquariums are. I keep the ceiling light off, so the tank lights shine brightly. My fish look like they're under spotlights, dancing in waves of light.

I like to turn the lights off in my room and watch the fish with just the tank lights on.

I like the sound of the water trickling through the filters. My mom thinks the filters are noisy. But the purring sound makes me feel calm and relaxed. Sometimes I clean my tanks or rearrange the rocks and stuff in them. Mostly I just sit and watch the fish. I really love keeping fish.

I have six tanks in the bedroom I share with Stefan. Besides those, I take care of a big tank in the basement and smaller ones in the living room and in Bjorn's room. Altogether, I have about 75 fish. As you can see, fishkeeping has become a big part of my life!

My brother Stefan likes fish, too. But I'm the one who does most of the work!

I talked to my family about getting a dog or cat, but Mom and Dad didn't think those pets would be the best for us.

I got my first fish aquarium a couple of years ago. I'd been wanting to get a pet. At first I thought it would be fun to have a dog or a cat or even a rabbit. But we have a pretty full house, and our yard is too small for animals. For me, fish were just right. They are peaceful, fun to watch, and not too demanding. You don't have to walk them or pet them. And they don't take up much space.

I first learned about fishkeeping from my friend Chad. Chad and his parents used to be our next-door neighbors, and Chad practically became a member of our family. Then Chad moved to an apartment nearby. He takes classes at the university and works at a fish store.

Parts of a fish

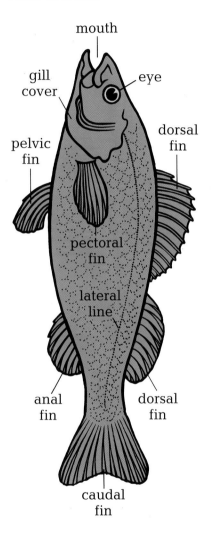

mouth

gill
cover

eye

pelvic
fin

dorsal
fin

pectoral
fin

lateral
line

anal
fin

dorsal
fin

caudal
fin

Chad always kept fish when he lived next door. Sometimes he let me help him with his aquariums. I loved to watch the big goldfish in Chad's tank in the den. My favorite fish to feed were the big ones in the cichlid *(SICK-lid)* tank. Cichlids are mostly freshwater fish with flattish bodies and spiky fins. To feed them, I'd hold a piece of food about an inch above the water. Then the fish would jump up to grab the food from my fingers. I could even feel their little teeth poking, but it didn't hurt.

Chad had one aquarium filled with lots of different water plants and grasses—pearl grasses, ferns, large-leafed plants, and bushy plants. The leaves made plenty of hiding places for the guppies that swam around in them.

Cichlids like to nip and chase each other. They're fun to watch.

Chad has taught me a lot about fish.

Chad also kept a community tank. That's an aquarium with a variety of fish in it. Chad had danios, tetras, mollies, loaches, and a plecostomus. Danios are small, active fish that swim near the top of the water. Tetras are also small. They travel in groups called schools. Mollies are small to medium sized, with a large dorsal fin on top of the back. Loaches are bottom-feeding fish—they eat the leftover food that sinks down into the gravel. Some of them are long and look like worms. Others, like the clown loach, are rounder, with pointy mouths. Plecostomuses are a kind of catfish. They eat algae.

Freshwater Setups

Almost all freshwater aquariums contain some basic things, such as gravel, water, fish, and decorations. But the huge variety of fish, plants, and decorations available makes it possible to create a wide range of tank habitats. Most fishkeepers start out with some type of community tank—an aquarium that houses several compatible fish species, with some plants, wood, or rocks for decoration and shelter. Other setups feature a single species or a group of fish that are similar. Still other tanks contain mostly plants, with few or no fish.

Fishkeepers set up tanks with just one species when they want a pair of fish to spawn, or breed. Sometimes certain fish are kept in their own tanks because they do not get along with other fish. For example, male betta fish will fight any other fish they live with, so they are most often kept alone in small tanks or bowls. Cichlids are very popular tropical freshwater fish that are usually kept in their own tanks. Cichlids often dig up plants, so their aquariums usually are furnished with rocks, wood, or pottery for shelter.

Different kinds of fish also require different water temperatures. Most fish need to be in warm water. Others can handle a wide temperature range. Goldfish can be kept without heaters. Koi, a colorful carp, also thrive in colder water. It's best to keep koi in garden pools because of their large size. Some tropical fish prefer brackish water—a mixture of fresh and saltwater.

Aquarium setups can feature a dazzling array of plants. Plant tanks can resemble gardens, ponds, streams, or grassy prairies. Some have driftwood and rocks. Usually, the fish in a plant tank are quite small. Some plant tanks have no fish.

The range of decorations for aquariums is also wide. Castles, divers, rocks, bottles, shells, and driftwood are just some possibilities.

Some days, I helped Chad with aquarium maintenance. We cleaned the tanks and filters, changed the water, and tested the water quality. When Chad and his parents went on vacation, they asked me to take care of the tanks. Every day, I went over to feed the fish. I also checked to make sure they all looked healthy. When the water in a tank seemed low, I added some.

One day Chad asked if I'd ever thought about getting an aquarium of my own. I had thought about it, but I wondered if I could take care of it by myself. Mom and Dad are busy, so I would have to be responsible for keeping the fish healthy. Chad thought I would do fine. He said I already knew just about all I needed to know about aquariums.

Chad said he would help me set up an aquarium of my own.

I was excited. Chad said he had an extra tank I could have. It was a 20-gallon tank—roomy enough but not too big to manage. I just needed to get the other equipment. Then Chad would help me set up the system. I could get the other stuff I needed at the fish store where Chad worked.

I asked my mom if it was okay. "That sounds like a great idea," Mom said. "It's something for you to do on your own, without your brothers."

I had saved enough money from my allowance to cover most of the cost of the equipment—filter, lights, heater, thermometer, water testing kit. I'd also need gravel and rocks, wood, or other decorations for inside the tank. Mom said that she and Dad would pitch in for the fish.

Chad gave me a 20-gallon aquarium, and my mom said she would buy the fish. I would pay for the rest of the equipment myself.

It's important to give a new aquarium time to go through the nitrogen cycle. Starting out with too many fish causes problems.

I wouldn't be getting many fish just yet, though. It takes a couple of weeks for a new aquarium to complete the nitrogen cycle. During the nitrogen cycle, materials in the tank, such as fish waste or leftover food, break down into their chemical parts. One of these chemicals is ammonia. Ammonia can kill fish. Normally, bacteria in the tank and the filter dissolve the ammonia quickly. But in a new tank, that bacteria hasn't formed yet. The bacteria forms from the waste of fish and other things in the tank. Starting with just a few fish in the tank allows the bacteria to build up slowly.

Mom talked to Chad and arranged for us to go to the fish store on Saturday to buy the things I needed. I could hardly wait!

I set up my first aquarium...

The fish store is one of my favorite places to hang out.

When Saturday finally arrived, we set off for A World of Fish. I had been there lots of times with Chad. It's a really cool place. I like to walk through the dark, tank-filled rooms and listen to the hum of filters, lights, and bubbles. The store carries a ton of different products. I didn't know where to start. Chad helped us pick out the right equipment for a 20-gallon freshwater aquarium.

One of the most important pieces in an aquarium is the filter. Filters remove bits of uneaten food, fish feces, and other matter. They also break down ammonia and nitrites—nitrites are another waste product that harms fish. Basically, filters keep the tank clean.

We bought a heater and a filter. There were a lot of different kinds of filters, but Chad helped me choose the right one.

A lot of filters are powered by air pumps. Pumps keep water moving around the tank and through the filter. We got a sponge filter that goes inside the tank. The air pump that powers the filter stays outside the tank. The pump and filter are connected by a long piece of tubing.

We bought a heater, because I wanted tropical (warm-water) fish. Some fish, like goldfish, don't need heat. I also picked out a net, a thermometer, some gravel, and a couple of lava rocks. We also bought some chemicals, a water-testing kit, and a couple of plastic plants. Later I would experiment with live plants. First I wanted to concentrate on caring for my fish. I didn't want to worry about plants, too.

Equipment Checklist

- **Tank**
  Some of the most common aquarium sizes are 10-gallon, 20-gallon, 35-gallon, 50-gallon, 75-gallon, and 125-gallon. The larger the tank, the more expensive—not only the aquarium, but also all the equipment needed to run it. But smaller tanks can be more difficult to maintain. A 10-gallon aquarium is the smallest size recommended for beginning fishkeepers. All-glass tanks are by far the most popular among fishkeepers.

- **Stand**
  Many setups come with stands that match the tanks. If you buy the aquarium and stand separately, make sure the stand is large enough to hold the entire tank bottom. The stand must also be sturdy enough to support the weight of the full tank.

- **Light hood and bulbs**
  A variety of light bulbs are available, ranging in price from a couple of dollars to more than $100 for some metal halide bulbs. Fish just need enough light to see, but plants do best under fluorescent bulbs.

- **Tank top or cover**
  If the light hood doesn't cover the entire top of the tank, you will need a glass cover. Many glass tank tops have hinges in the center, so half of the cover can be lifted to feed the fish.

- **Heater (for all tropical fish)**
- **Thermostat (if heater doesn't have one)**
- **Filter**
  Many types of filters are available. The most common are undergravel filters, internal power filters, and external "hang-on" power filters. Any of these is fine, as long as it is big enough for the tank.

- **Furnishings—gravel, wood, rocks, plants, other decorations**
- **Food**
- **Testing kits and additives**
- **Cleaning supplies—siphon, magnetic or brush cleaner, bucket**
- **Net**

A typical aquarium setup

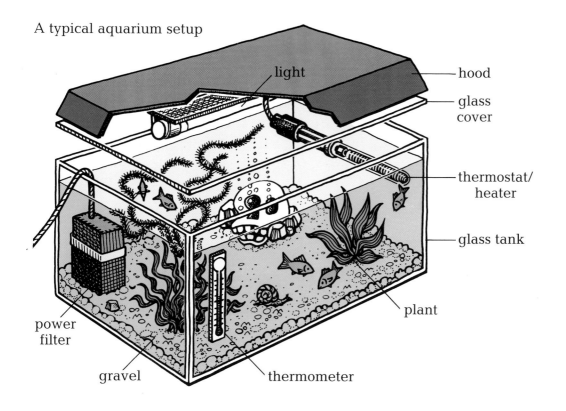

light — hood

glass cover

thermostat/ heater

glass tank

plant

power filter

gravel   thermometer

Altogether, we spent about $85. We saved some money by not having to buy an aquarium. That would have cost another $40 or more. Many new fishkeepers buy complete setups, which include the tank, a top, and lights. The top, or light hood, is what covers the tank and holds the light bulbs. Sometimes the top and light hood are separate. A glass top covers the tank, and a light hood holds the light bulbs above the glass.

We came home with a lot of stuff. Stefan was kind of shocked. He said, "Wow, Leif, what are you gonna do—make a pond?"

I rinsed the gravel under running water to clean it. The tank needed washing, too.

Dad found a stand in the garage and cleaned it up for me. He made sure it was strong enough to support an aquarium full of water—a full 20-gallon tank weighs up to 200 pounds!

Before I started to set up the aquarium, I washed it out really well with water. Then I lifted it onto the stand. Before pouring in the gravel, I washed it, too. That gets rid of all the dust, which can cloud the water. I poured the gravel so it sloped up toward the back of the tank.

I set the clean aquarium on the stand. Even without the water in it, the tank was pretty heavy! Then I poured the washed gravel in.

I wanted to include some decorations besides what the store had. Chad said that I could use all kinds of things—interesting rocks or pieces of wood, old bottles, clay pots. I just had to wash and boil whatever I wanted to use, to make sure everything was clean. You can clean plastic gravel or decorations by washing them in a mild solution of water and bleach.

I boiled a big rock I wanted to use in the tank. When everything was ready, Chad and I arranged things in the aquarium.

I decided on a twisted chunk of driftwood and some cool rocks. I found them on vacation last summer, when we went to the Oregon coast.

After everything was clean, I arranged the items in my tank. Then I planted the water plants. I pushed the roots into the gravel. I took my time landscaping my aquarium, because I wanted to do a good job. I wanted it to be a comfortable and interesting place for my pet fish to live.

The jugs of water were heavy, too. It took a while to fill the tank.

Next Chad and I added jugs of water from the tap. To keep from disturbing the gravel, we poured the water into a small plastic container at the bottom of the tank.

Finally, I placed the light hood on top and turned on the switch. Everyone cheered. It looked great!

The next day, Chad helped me set up the sponge filter.

The next day, Chad came over again to help me set up the filter and the rest of the equipment. First we added a neutralizer to get rid of any chlorine, ammonia, or chloramine. These chemicals are added to tap water. They kill germs and make the water safe to drink. But chlorine can be poisonous to fish. We set up the power filter, the heater, and the thermometer at the back of the aquarium. We didn't want them to be seen from the front. It was easy to hide them behind the plants and rocks.

The Nitrogen Cycle

Whenever you introduce fish or plants to an aquarium, you begin a process of chemical reaction called the nitrogen cycle. All living things create waste as they live and grow. Fish poop. Broken-off plant leaves decay. Unused food or fertilizer builds up. In a continuous cycle in nature, bacteria help break down the decomposing material into its chemical parts. Much of the waste is converted to ammonia. At high levels, ammonia is harmful to fish. Bacteria turn ammonia into nitrites, which can also be poisonous to fish. As the cycle continues, nitrites are finally converted to nitrates. Nitrates are less dangerous. They tend to disappear rapidly, because plants use them.

In a new aquarium, bacteria haven't formed yet. Ammonia levels can skyrocket and remain high until the bacteria that keep them in check have time to grow. The same thing can happen with nitrites. The bacteria that break them down also have not developed.

There are two ways you can avoid problems during the nitrogen cycle:

1. A few hardy fish, such as danios and tetras, can withstand high levels of ammonia and nitrites. Introducing a couple of small fish like these after you set up your tank will create some waste, or organic nitrogen, to break down. Ammonia and nitrite levels will rise, but the cycle won't be as extreme as if lots of fish were introduced. And because the new fish are especially hardy, they should survive the process.

2. A water additive made especially for new tanks can be added to a new aquarium. The additive contains live bacteria. In a few days, they will become established. With bacteria in place, the ammonia and nitrites will break down more quickly.

Daily water testing can keep you informed about where your new aquarium is in the nitrogen cycle. When ammonia levels and nitrite levels have peaked and then fallen away, you can feel safe in adding fish—but not many at a time. Every additional fish means more fish waste. Adding lots of fish at the same time creates high levels of ammonia and nitrites.

I started with just a few danios in my new aquarium. They would be able to survive the nitrogen cycle.

Then Chad brought over a few zebra danios. They are fish that can survive in a tank during the nitrogen cycle. I would have to wait a couple of weeks before I could get any more fish. Otherwise, the ammonia produced in the nitrogen cycle could make them sick or even kill them.

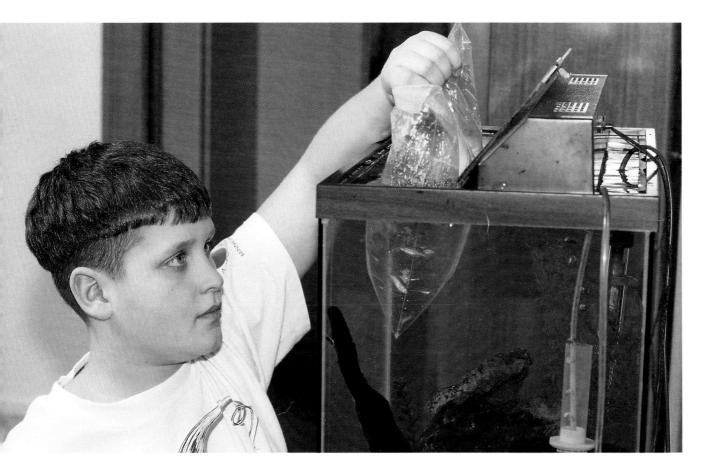

It was time to pick out my new fish...

Chad suggested that I read some books so I would know what kind of fish to get.

It was hard to wait those two weeks. To pass the time, I read some fish books that Chad lent me. Learning about the different varieties of fish helps you decide which kinds you might like to have in your tank. Chad told me to check to see how big the different kinds of fish get and how they behave. I also needed to make sure the fish I chose would get along. Some fish like to be alone. Others swim in groups. Some fish are shy and sleep during the day. Others are active during the day. If you put fish together that have different habits, they might fight, get sick, or even die.

Cycling a new tank can take anywhere from two to six weeks. While I waited, I read books about fish, kept an eye on the danios, and tested the water.

After speeding through Chad's books, I asked Mom to take me to the library to check out some more. My favorite fish books are the atlases. Each one has hundreds of color photos of every type of fish you could imagine. Did you know there are over 20,000 species of fish in the world? Of course, you can't buy all these fish at fish stores. Some are endangered species, and it's against the law to keep them in a private home.

Every day, I watched the danios. I tested the water with the testing kit we bought at the store. The test shows the level of ammonia and nitrites in the aquarium. As the nitrogen cycle progresses, the amount of ammonia in the water peaks and then falls. Nitrite levels then fall.

Water Testing and Additives

Maintaining good water quality is one of a fishkeeper's most important jobs. Along with cleaning the tank and changing the water, regular water tests will help keep the aquarium water clean and healthy. An easy way to remember when to do a water test is to do it when you make water changes, every two weeks or so.

One of the most basic tests is a pH test. The pH values range from 0 (very acidic) to 14 (very alkaline). A pH of 7 is neutral. Aquarium test kits usually give a measurement from 5 to 9, because the pH values of any water very rarely fall outside these levels. For a community tank, the pH should be between 6.6 and 7.4. Some fish, like many African cichlids, prefer more alkaline water, with a pH of about 7.8. Other types of fish like more acidic water.

The pH testing kit will either provide drops that are added to a test tube full of aquarium water, or a paper strip that's dipped into the test tube. The test-tube water or the paper strip will change color. The color is then compared with colors on a chart. Each color corresponds with a pH value. Most kits also include drops to add to aquarium water to increase or decrease the pH as needed.

Other water tests can tell you how much ammonia or nitrites are in the aquarium water. A salinity test, used mostly for saltwater tanks, tells the salt content of the water. Many additional tests are available, but these are usually unnecessary for beginners.

It was fun looking at all the fish, knowing I was finally going to buy some.

After two weeks, the water was cleared of excess ammonia and nitrites. And my danios had done fine. The tank was ready for more fish. Thanks to all my research, I knew what kinds of fish I wanted. I hoped the store would have them.

Mom, Chad, and I went to the fish store again. It was even more fun this time, now that I actually got to pick out fish. I explained to Chad and another store clerk what I wanted. "I'm interested in tiger barbs, dwarf gouramies, and platies," I said.

"Oh," Chad said, "you mean goo-RAH-mies?"

I laughed. I'd said "GOR-a-mies." How was I supposed to know how to say it? Fish have some pretty strange names.

"I'd also like to get a sucker fish," I said. Sucker fish, like plecostamuses (plecos) and other catfish, eat the algae that grows on the inner walls of the tank, on rocks, and on anything else inside the aquarium.

Chad showed me the barbs, gouramies, and platies. He recommended that I get at least four tiger barbs, because they do better in groups than as singles or in pairs. We also decided on a pair of dwarf flame gouramies. They're really pretty. The male has bright reddish orange and blue stripes, and the female is golden colored with less noticeable stripes.

I wanted to get some tiger barbs and gouramies.

I also picked out a brown loach that was hiding in the plants. When it was time to buy food, I didn't know where to start. Chad helped me pick out a couple different kinds of fish food.

As we were picking out a small pleco, I noticed some brown loaches swimming around and around in a nearby tank. They had long skinny bodies and cute whiskers. They seemed to be having a lot of fun. I chose one of those, too. Chad said that was plenty of fish to start with. My fish would grow, and I shouldn't overcrowd my tank.

After choosing the fish, we looked at the food. The store had frozen food, dried food, and live food. In the freezer, there were shrimp, krill, and bloodworms. For dry foods, the basic choices were spirulina flakes, freeze-dried worms, brine shrimp and plankton, and algae wafers. They also had pellets, flakes, and morsels of mixed foods designed for specific types of fish.

When you buy fish, the store puts them in a plastic bag filled with water and oxygen.

Next, Chad used a net to scoop up the fish I'd picked out. He put them in plastic bags and filled the bags halfway up with water. Then he added oxygen from an oxygen tank to each plastic bag. "That keeps the fish comfortable until you can introduce them to your aquarium," Chad explained. Mom paid for the fish and the food—it all cost about $50.

When we got home, we lifted up the light hood and floated the plastic bags in the aquarium water. Before being let loose in the water, the fish need to get used to the temperature. The danios swam around the bags—I'm sure they wondered what was going on! After a few minutes, we opened each bag to allow some of the aquarium water to mix with the water inside the bag. Then we coaxed the fish out of the bags as we pulled the bags out of the water.

My fish arrived at their home!

At first, the new fish seemed nervous. The gouramies, the pleco, and the loach hid behind the rocks, wood, and plants. The barbs swam around nervously, along with the danios. But soon they all seemed to get used to their new surroundings and tankmates. Before long, all the fish were swimming around the tank. They didn't seem a bit nervous. Even the loach was swimming happily in his squirmy, wiggly way.

I showed off my new pets to my family.

I learned not to overfeed my fish...

Every day I fed my fish—a pinch in the morning and another bit at night. I varied the food I gave them so they would get the nutrients and flavors they needed to stay healthy and happy. I also checked the ammonia level in the aquarium by testing the water each day. Chad told me that ammonia can build up fast after introducing several new fish into a new aquarium. If the ammonia level rose, my fish could be in trouble.

To test the water, I scoop some from the tank into a small vial. Then I add a drop of one chemical, and seven drops from each of the other two chemicals. (The chemicals and the vial came with the testing kit.)

Chad taught me to feed the fish only as much as they would eat in five minutes.

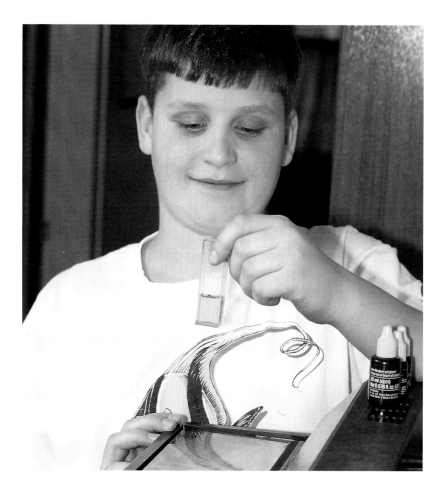

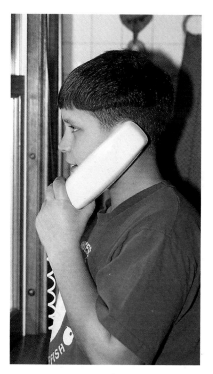

I tested the water every day, but one day something was wrong. I called Chad.

For the first few days, everything seemed to be going perfectly. The fish seemed happy and ate all their food, and the water tested okay. Then one day I came home from school and I knew something was wrong. The barbs and gouramies looked tired and weak. They just sat there instead of swimming around. The danios swam slowly near the top. I couldn't even find the pleco or the loach. I called Chad.

Chad said to test the ammonia, nitrite, and pH levels and that he'd be right over. By the time he got there, I was reading the test results—the ammonia had skyrocketed. Chad and I did a water change. We replaced about one-third of the aquarium's water with fresh tap water. First we drained water from the tank into a bucket using a siphon (a siphon is like a big hose). Then we used the siphon to add the new water from a bucket to the tank. Chad added some chemicals to bring down the ammonia level and to make the tap water safe for the fish. Then there was nothing to do but wait.

We added a chemical to the aquarium to bring down the ammonia level. I found out that too much food can hurt fish.

Overfeeding can lead to a buildup of waste at the bottom of the tank.

The next morning, my fish looked a lot better. I sprinkled in a pinch of food. When they all ate hungrily, I was relieved. I had caught the problem before my fish were seriously hurt.

After that, I was careful not to feed my fish too much. I knew that too much food causes ammonia to build up, because the uneaten food falls to the bottom of the tank and decomposes. I also learned that changing the tank water with fresh water every two weeks or so keeps the environment healthy for the fish. Good filtration and a clean tank and filter are also important.

I use the siphon to change the tank water. I start by draining about one-fourth of the water. When taking out the water, I use the end of the siphon to suck all the gunk—debris, food, feces—from the gravel. Then I fill the tank with fresh water, and add a solution that takes the chlorine out of the tap water.

I change the water and clean my tank every couple of weeks. It takes about 20 minutes.

After I drain about one-fourth of the water with the siphon, I add fresh water. The magnetic scrubber is easy to use. I don't even get my hands wet!

Each time I change the water, I also clean the tank and filter. First I scrub the inside walls of the tank with a magnetic cleaner. I hold on to one part of the magnet on the outside of the glass. The other part of the magnet stays on the inside of the glass. The inside magnet is a scrubber. It cleans the glass as it moves along with the magnet piece in my hand. Then I use another scrubber—a spongy brush with a handle—to get in the corners and other hard-to-reach spots. To clean the filter, I either siphon the water from it, or I take it out and squeeze it in the sink and rinse it out.

Fish Diseases

If you change and test your aquarium water regularly, have a good filter, and do not overcrowd the tank, your fish will likely stay healthy. The most common cause of disease in fish is stress. Several things can stress fish, including poor water quality, changes in water temperature, too many fish or incompatible species in a tank, the wrong water temperature or pH, the wrong foods, and not enough hiding places.

Some signs that your fish might be sick include
- fins held unusually close to the body
- fins rotting
- the fish doesn't eat for more than two days
- white spots on the fish
- the fish gasps at the surface of the water
- a normally active fish slows down, or a normally still fish is active
- the fish is bloated (puffy looking)

One of the most common diseases among freshwater fish is *ich* (pronounced ICK). Fish with ich have little white spots on them, and the fish may scratch against objects in the tank. Ich is a parasite (a tiny bug) that collects on the fins and gills of fish. As the spots fall off, they reproduce. The parasites can affect all of the fish in a tank. Ich can be treated with a medicine that is available at fish stores. You put a few drops of medicine in the tank each day until the disease is gone, which usually takes about a week.

If you think your fish is sick, you can talk to someone at a pet store about what kind of medicine to buy or what else to do.

I test the water in my tank every week. The pH test is one of the most important.

I also keep up my habit of testing the water to make sure it has the right pH value and the right chemical balance. The pH value has to do with how hard or soft the water is. Most of my fish prefer a neutral pH—neither alkaline water nor acidic water. Tap water varies from city to city. Our water is pretty good—just a little on the acidic side. I can raise the pH by adding a few drops of an adjustment solution.

Fishkeeping involves a lot of technical stuff. It's almost like a science project at times, like chemistry. That's part of what makes it fun.

I wanted to try something new...

I've been helping out a lot at A World of Fish. When I turn 16, I want to get a part-time job there.

After a while, I began to feel like a pro at fishkeeping. I read even more books about aquarium fish. And I've spent so much time at A World of Fish that they even let me help out sometimes. I feed the fish, clean tanks, and put oxygen into bags for customers.

At home, Bjorn and Stefan have become fish fans, too. Bjorn likes to feed the fish. Stefan likes watching the danios, because they move so fast.

African cichlids are popular aquarium fish, but they are becoming endangered in their natural habitat of the Rift lakes.

After reading some articles in a magazine, I wanted to try something new—cichlids. African cichlids come from the African Rift lakes, the big lakes in east central Africa. Other African cichlids are found throughout much of Africa. Close cousins of the African cichlids live in Central America, South America, and parts of Asia.

The greatest thing about cichlids is how pretty they are. They have long, flowing fins and sleek bodies. They come in a rainbow of colors. Cichlids definitely have a personality, too. They are feisty fish that chase and nip at each other. They fight to be "tank boss." They dig up plants and take apart rock or wood arrangements.

I bought two new kinds of filters—a canister filter, which sits below the aquarium, and an external biowheel filter.

Because my 20-gallon aquarium was already almost too full of fish, I needed another tank. I decided to get a 30-gallon tank. I would put cichlids in it, plus a few of the fish from my 20-gallon tank. That way, the fish left in the smaller tank would have more room to grow. I could put the loach, the danios, and the pleco in with the new cichlids.

I dug into my savings again and bought a used 30-gallon aquarium, a canister filter, an external filter, a heater, and a top with lights. I didn't bother getting any plants, since the cichlids would just dig them up. Chad gave me some gravel and rocks he wasn't using. I was set.

Filters

Some of the most common types of filters include the following.

- **Undergravel filter.** This inexpensive filter is a plastic plate with rows of tiny holes. It sits on a raised platform, fitting the bottom of the aquarium. Two tubes rise from the plate. One is the intake. The other has a powerhead (a small electric water pump). It pulls the water up from the filter and pushes it out a spout. Some undergravel filters use an air pump that sits outside the tank.
- **External (*or hang-on*) filter.** The external filter straps onto the back of the aquarium. An intake tube draws water into the filter. The water flows through filter media, such as carbon or polyester, and then back out into the tank through a wide, traylike outlet or over a turning wheel. External filters are easy to use.
- **Canister filter.** Self-powered, a canister filter can also work with an external filter. An intake tube draws water from the tank into the canister, which sits outside the tank. The water moves through the canister's chambers and then out another tube. The water can then be directed through tubing back into the tank or through another filter. The type of filter media used in the canister can be changed.
- **Internal filter.** This is an inexpensive filter that sits in a corner of the aquarium. Usually powered by a powerhead or an air pump, an internal filter contains filter media, such as a sponge.
- **Trickle (*or wet-dry*) filter.** Generally used with saltwater systems, the trickle filter sits under an aquarium. The filter is powered by a heavy-duty water pump that forces water up into the tank. Strapped on the back of the tank is a prefilter, which drains water from the tank down to the filter through plastic tubing. The water is released over a large tray that has rows of small holes. Then the water trickles over a large bin full of plastic spiky balls. The bacteria that filter the water grow on these balls. The water then flows through a thick sponge into the next compartment, where the water pump sits.

There are lots of different types of African cichlids. I don't even know all their names.

I set up the new tank in my bedroom. I thought about what would make the best home for cichlids. African cichlids need water with a high pH value. Some need special foods. Most are very territorial, so they need their own space. You have to give them plenty of resting and hiding spots.

For my aquarium, I got two *Neolamprologus brichardi* (daffodil cichlids), two *Neolamprologus brevis,* and two *Julidochromis ornatus.* All of these cichlids are from Lake Tanganyika. I've learned that it's best to keep cichlids from just one African lake together in an aquarium. Varieties from other lakes need a different quality of water.

Daffodils like to hide, sleep, and breed in caves. I made two cavelike places for mine, using curved pieces of clay pots and clay tubes. The brevis fish are shell-dwellers. I got a couple of large empty snail shells at the fish store for them. The *Julidochromis* also like to hide in caves or shells.

I loved my new tank. Besides the new cichlids, the loach, the pleco, and a couple danios lived in the 30-gallon tank. I made sure there were places for all of them to hide—in the rocks, under clay pots, inside shells. They all seemed to be thriving. The daffodils constantly defended their territory—the little caves.

Many fish like to hide behind rocks or in caves. When I add a new fish to a tank, the fish usually hides at first.

Some fish, like mollies, give birth to live babies. These fish are called live-bearers. Other fish, such as cichlids, lay eggs. After my fish bred, I moved some fish to a new tank.

After school one day, I sat on my bed to watch the fish in the cichlid tank. I hadn't seen much of the daffodils for a couple of days. This day they were out, carefully guarding the space around the clay pot they called home. I took a closer look. Swimming around the openings in the clay pieces were 10, 20, 30, or more tiny baby fish! Without even trying, I had succeeded in breeding fish!

I decided I needed another aquarium. For Christmas, my parents gave me another 30-gallon tank.

Baby fish, called fry, are so tiny. But they grow, of course, so once again I needed a new aquarium. This time I bought a 55-gallon tank. I set it up in the basement.

As they grew, the daffodil fry (babies) got braver. They explored every corner of the aquarium. By the time they were about a half-inch long, I could count about 25 of them. Not long after, I spotted another batch of tiny fry. The pair had bred again. The babies were so cute and helpless looking—just pairs of eyes swimming around the entrance to their clay home.

I realized I couldn't keep all the babies in the tank, and I couldn't let the pair keep breeding more. I looked in the newspaper classified ads and found a secondhand 55-gallon aquarium. I bought it and put in as many larger babies as I could catch. Later, I put in the second batch of babies, plus the female parent. When the fry were large enough, I took some of them to the fish store to be sold. I knew that they were healthy. They would find good homes with other aquarists.

Then I had another problem to solve. The tank that housed the male daffodil, the loach, and the danios was getting direct sunlight for part of the day. Sunlight helps algae to grow. Without the pleco to eat the algae, the tank's inside walls slowly became coated with a thin layer of blue-green, slimy algae. I changed the water, scraped the walls, and got a new algae-eating pleco.

When one of my tanks started getting covered with mucky green algae, I bought a new pleco. They are called sucker fish because they suck all the gunk off the tank walls.

My most recent project is a saltwater tank...

Stefan loves his piranhas.

For Stefan's eighth birthday, I set up a 10-gallon aquarium in our bedroom for him. Stefan wanted piranhas, so we got two little ones. In the wild, piranhas live in large schools, or groups. They grow to be very big. They are attracted to the smell of blood and can quickly tear apart other fish, birds, and even mammals. Some piranhas will even attack each other. You have to make sure to get two that will get along.

Stefan's piranhas are small, but they still like live food. He feeds them rosy minnows. We buy 12 or 20 minnows at a time when we go to the fish store. Stefan loves his fish tank and feeds the fish every day. He gets so excited watching them eat. "Look!" he yells. "The piranha ate the head off the minnow!" I help him out by doing the water changes and cleanings.

One of my favorite tanks in our bedroom has two angelfish. Angelfish come from the Amazon River system in South America. They are relatives of African cichlids. Angelfish are graceful swimmers with round, flat bodies and very long, flowing fins. I don't keep any other fish in the angelfish tank. The angels bully smaller fish, and larger fish may bite the angelfishes' fins.

Angelfish are very mellow fish. They swim slowly.

My most recent aquarium project is a saltwater tank. I have been reading up on saltwater fish and other creatures, such as snails, crabs, sea horses, and corals. It is all so cool—but so complicated! Besides pH, ammonia, and chlorine, you have to worry about how much salt is in the water, saltwater diseases, and other things.

I talked to my mom about my plans, and she had a great idea. Someone had donated a 55-gallon aquarium to the Emerson School. That's where I go to school—I'm in sixth grade. My mom also works there part-time, doing public relations and other things. She asked me if I would like to set up my saltwater system at school, so lots of kids could enjoy it. I said sure! She asked the principal if it was okay, and she agreed. My mom and I decided we would take care of the tank together.

Saltwater fish, like butterfly fish and blue tangs, are so cool!

Saltwater Aquariums

Saltwater, or marine, aquariums, are a challenge to set up and maintain, but they can house some of the most beautiful, brightly colored fish in the world. Other saltwater setups feature corals, live rocks, and invertebrates such as anemones, shrimps, crabs, and sea urchins. Saltwater tanks require more maintenance than freshwater setups.

Experts recommend setting up either fish-only tanks or reef tanks. A reef tank contains a combination of live rock, corals, and other creatures found naturally in shallow-water habitats. Live rock is any type of limestone or dead coral skeleton that has been taken over by bacteria, algae, sponges, and other small creatures, including sea squirts and sea anemones. Besides being fascinating to watch, live rock houses bacteria that break down ammonia and turn nitrates into harmless gasses.

Besides live rock, a reef tank can contain a variety of corals, including brain coral, elegance coral, and leather coral. The corals and invertebrates on live rock require special lighting to thrive. The lighting that best mimics natural reef sunlight is metal halide lighting. Metal halide bulbs are expensive, but they are necessary to keep reef creatures healthy. Reef systems also require additives such as calcium, which can be found in a high-quality fish store. Reef systems do best with protein skimmers and denitrifying filters. Protein skimmers, which hang on the back of the tank, remove organic waste.

Fish-only saltwater setups require slightly less maintenance, but still must be well monitored. With average lighting and a trickle filter, a saltwater fish tank requires only regular water changes and water testing. As with freshwater fish, it is important not to crowd the aquarium with too many fish. The tank should include rocks so that the fish have places to sleep or hide.

I wanted to experiment with some corals, so I had to go with a pretty high-tech filter. I chose a trickle filter to start with. There are other kinds of saltwater filters. I probably will need another kind at some point. Corals and live rocks need powerful lighting. I know that light bulbs called metal halide bulbs work best. Chad keeps his metal halide lights in a light hood he built above his saltwater tank.

Some of my friends are into fish, too. We all take an interest in the school aquarium.

Corals and sea anemones
require strong lights.

After I assembled the saltwater aquarium, I waited a few weeks to allow the good kind of bacteria to build up. Then I introduced a few blennies to help cycle the tank (assist in the nitrogen cycle). Later, I added a maroon clownfish, a royal gramma, lots of different kinds of coral, and an arrow crab. So far, my saltwater aquarium is doing fine. We have it in the library at school, so all the kids get to see it.

I'm still trying to decide what else to put in the tank. I've learned that it's best to keep coral and invertebrates separate from fish, so I might have to get a new saltwater aquarium just for fish. Then I could get anything . . . a sea anemone with waving tentacles like arms . . . a shrimp that looks like a candy cane . . . sea urchins, mollusks, sea worms, tangs, gobies, wrasses, triggerfish, parrotfish, anemonefish, puffers, angelfish, butterfly fish. . . . I have a lot of choices!

All of these saltwater creatures are beautiful and unique. They are also hard to care for. Corals and other invertebrates are especially hard. With a saltwater tank, you need to change and test the water a lot, at least once a week. The fish have special feeding needs. But I'm always learning more, so I know I can do it.

I still like to hole up in my bedroom and watch the fish in my freshwater tanks. My mom and dad thought I'd get bored with aquariums, but they were wrong. The more I've learned, the more I want to find out about fishkeeping. I don't think I'll ever get bored with it.

Now I can't imagine home without my fish. Stefan and Bjorn and my mom and dad really like them, too. I guess my fish family will just keep getting bigger!

I'm glad I decided to start keeping fish. They are the best pet for me.

Glossary

Ammonia (uh-*moh*-nyuh): a chemical produced when waste and other matter break down. Ammonia can be deadly to fish.

Aquarist (uh-*kwair*-ist): a person who keeps an aquarium

Canister filter: a cylinder-shaped filter that sits outside the aquarium

Chlorine (*klor*-een): a gas that is added to tap water to kill germs

Community tank: an aquarium that houses several compatible species of fish

Fry: baby fish

Ich: (ick): an abbreviation of *Ichthyopthirius multifiliis;* a common parasite that collects on the fins and gills of fish

Invertebrate (in-*vur*-tuh-brit): a creature without a backbone, such as a snail, crab, or coral

Live-bearer: fish that give birth to live young, rather than laying eggs

Live rock: limestone or dead coral skeletons on which bacteria, algae, sponges, and other small creatures live

Nitrates (*nye*-trates): substances released during the nitrogen cycle

Nitrites (*nye*-trites): substances released during the nitrogen cycle

Nitrogen (*nye*-truh-juhn) **cycle:** a process in which waste materials in a tank are broken down into their chemical parts

pH value: a measurement of how acidic or alkaline water is

Protein (*pro*-teen) **skimmer:** a filter that forms a stream of bubbles that catch protein from the water

Territorial (*ter*-uh-toh-ree-uhl): fish that claim a certain area, or territory, in a tank and defend it by threatening other fish who come too close

Trickle filter: A filter used in saltwater tanks that sits outside the tank and pumps the water over spiky balls. A trickle filter is sometimes called a wet-dry filter.

Resources

American Aquarist Society, Inc.
Box 100
3901 Hatch Blvd.
Sheffield, AL 35660
(205) 386-7687

Federation of American Aquarium Societies
923 Wadsworth
Syracuse, NY 13208

Marine Aquarium Societies of North America
948 Summit Lakeshore Rd. N.W.
Olympia, WA 98502

On the World Wide Web:

AquaLink
http://www.aqualink.com

AquaScape Aquarium Hobbyist Magazine
http://www.netservetech.com/AquaScapeMag.html

FINS (Fish Information Service)
http://WWW.ActWin.Com/fish/

FishNet
http://wso.williams.edu/~falarcon/fish/

For Further Reading

Evans, Mark. *Fish: A Practical Guide to Caring for Your Fish.* ASPCA Pet Care Guides for Kids. New York: Dorling Kindersley, 1993.

Mills, Dick. *Aquarium Fish.* Eyewitness Handbooks. New York: Dorling Kindersley, 1993.

Randolph, Elizabeth. *The Basic Book of Fish Keeping.* New York: Fawcett Crest, 1990.

Scheurmann, Ines. *Aquarium Plants Manual.* Hauppauge, New York: Barron's Educational Series, 1993.

Souza, D.M. *Fish That Play Tricks.* Minneapolis: Carolrhoda Books, 1998.

———. *Underwater Musicians.* Minneapolis: Carolrhoda Books, 1998.

Index

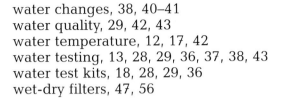

ABOUT THE AUTHOR

Lori Coleman lives in Eagan, Minnesota, with her husband, Pete, and daughter, Ginger. Other members of their household are Drake, a springer spaniel, Piper, a cocker spaniel, Sammy, a yellow Lab, and five fish tanks' worth of fish, including cichlids, plecos, loaches, blennies, and a large, friendly blue tang. Coleman also is the author of *Fundamental Soccer.*

ABOUT THE PHOTOGRAPHER

Jerry Boucher lives with his wife, Elaine, in an old brick country school in rural Amery, Wisconsin. He has worked for 30 years in photography, advertising, and graphic arts. His company, Schoolhouse Productions, does commercial photography, graphic design, and tourism brochures. The father of three sons, Boucher is also involved with Kinship, a teen photo group, and several arts organizations.